Geo. P. Bissell

Coin Book issued by the Banking House

Geo. P. Bissell

Coin Book issued by the Banking House

ISBN/EAN: 9783742826855

Manufactured in Europe, USA, Canada, Australia, Japa

Cover: Foto ©knipser5 / pixelio.de

Manufactured and distributed by brebook publishing software
(www.brebook.com)

Geo. P. Bissell

Coin Book issued by the Banking House

1873.

BANKING HOUSE

OF

GEORGE P. BISSELL & CO..

DEALERS IN

SAFE NINE PER CENT. BONDS,

GOVERNMENT SECURITIES,

AND

FIRST-CLASS INVESTMENTS,

HARTFORD, CONN.

Established in 1854, and conducted on the safe principles which govern
our best Savings-Banks.

HARTFORD:

1873.

ESTABLISHED 1854.

BANKING HOUSE

OF

GEORGE P. BISSELL & CO.

HARTFORD, January, 1873.

The undersigned are associated as Bankers in Hartford, Conn., under the name and style of GEO. P. BISSELL & CO., having an office of Discount and Deposit, and General Banking Business, at 309 Main Street.

They give their attention to furnishing safe investments for large or small amounts, the discounting and negotiation of Commercial Paper and Loans, making collections in all parts of the country, and buying and selling Exchange, Coin, and Drafts on Europe.

They will effect purchases and sales of Government Stocks, Bank Stocks, Railroad Shares and Bonds, and all other Stocks, Bonds, and Securities. Their facilities for buying and selling on commission at the New York Board are unsurpassed.

They will also act as agents for parties abroad, in the collection and payment of interest and dividends, and in the transaction of any Banking or Brokerage business.

They receive deposits, and *allow interest from the date of the deposit.*

The undersigned have had a long and successful experience in Banking, and they intend, in conducting their business, to exercise the utmost prudence and caution, so that their house shall rank second to no Private Banking establishment, Joint Stock Bank, Trust Company, or Savings-Bank, in the country, for soundness and stability.

GEORGE P. BISSELL,
EDWARD H. PERKINS.

☞ For SPECIAL and VALUABLE information about SAFE INVESTMENTS, see page 18.

Our Terms for Receiving Deposits.

WE offer the following advantages to all who open accounts with us:

1st. We receive any sum, from fifty dollars upward.

2d. WE PAY INTEREST FROM THE DATE OF DEPOSITS TILL THE DATE OF WITHDRAWAL. THIS IS A GREAT ADVANTAGE OVER THE SYSTEM OF QUARTER-DAYS ADOPTED BY SAVINGS-BANKS, BY WHICH DEPOSITORS LOSE THE INTEREST ON ALL MONEY DRAWN BETWEEN THE QUARTER-DAYS. *We give them the whole interest.*

3d. We add the interest to the principal on the 1st days of May and November.

4th. We allow interest, at a rate which may be agreed upon, on the current accounts of Merchants, Manufacturers, Contractors, Town Officers, Administrators of Estates, and others whose funds are active, receiving the money in large or small sums, and paying it out on checks, without notice,—just as the account would be kept at a Bank,—allowing interest on daily balances.

5th. *We conduct our business upon the safe principles which govern the best Savings-Banks;* and at the same time we have adopted all the improvements in Banking which have been adopted in the largest Banks and

PLATE I.

GOLD COINS OF THE UNITED STATES.

I. The Eagle—Ten Dollars. 1870.

II. Double Eagle—Twenty Dollars. 1870.

III. Half-Eagle—Five Dollars. 1870.

IV. Three Dollars. 1870.

V. Quarter-Eagle—$2 50. 1870.   VI. One Dollar. 1870.

PLATE I.

GOLD COINS OF THE UNITED STATES.

I. THE EAGLE—TEN DOLLARS.

WEIGHT, 258 Grains.

Fineness—900–1000.

II. DOUBLE EAGLE—TWENTY DOLLARS.

Authorized by Act of Congress, March 3, 1849.

WEIGHT, 516 Grains.

Fineness—900–1000.

III. HALF-EAGLE--FIVE DOLLARS. 1870.

Authorized by Act of Congress, 1837.

WEIGHT, 129 Grains.

Fineness—900–1000.

IV. THREE DOLLARS. 1870.

Authorized by Act of Congress, 1853.

WEIGHT, 774 Grains.

Fineness—900–1000.

V. QUARTER-EAGLE. 1870.--$2 50.

Authorized by Act of Congress, January 1837.

WEIGHT, 64½ Grains.

Fineness—900–1000.

VI. ONE DOLLAR. 1870.—$1.

Authorized by Act of Congress, March 3, 1849.

WEIGHT, 25.8 Grains.

Fineness—900–1000.

Banking Offices in New York and other cities; we are thus enabled to give facilities and extend a liberality to our customers which incorporated institutions cannot do. Another great advantage which we offer lies in the fact that we have no board of directors before whom the business affairs of our customers have to pass, and no stockholders, who, with the directors, have a right to examine the accounts of our depositors and dealers. We have but two partners, to whom alone the transactions with our house are known, and we make no reports of any kind to anybody. *We consider ourselves the confidential financial agents of our customers, and their affairs are never the subject of remarks or criticism.*

6th. Our customers who may desire information concerning Stocks and Bonds of any kind, or who may wish to be posted upon any matters in our line, may feel at liberty to write us at any time making such inquiries, and we will take great pleasure in giving all the information in our power.

7th. Our Capital is Ample,

And we have been established in Hartford, as Bankers, more than eighteen years, and although during that time there have been seasons of great financial disaster to the country (particularly in 1857 and 1860), we have conducted our business with such prudence and caution that we have met with no reverses, even in the worst panics in the money-market, and at no time have the interests of our depositors been jeopardized.

U. S. Securities a Specialty.

Our facilities are such, and we have such large transactions with the Government, and with dealers in New York, that we are able to give as good terms to our customers at our office in Hartford as they can get in New York, in the purchase and sale of United States securities, and all other Stocks and Bonds.

Our Comparative Strength.

Governor Jewell, in his message to the Legislature this spring, thus reviews the Trust Companies in this State:

"The most novel feature in our financial matters is the Trust Companies, of which there are five in the State, with a capital, all told, of five hundred and thirty-six thousand seven hundred and fifty dollars ($536,750), of which two hundred and forty thousand dollars ($240,000) are invested in real estate. These five institutions owed to depositors on the 1st of January, 1872, one million one hundred and nineteen thousand one hundred and forty-five dollars and forty-seven cents ($1,119,145.47), and show cash on hand the insignificant amount of forty-two thousand twenty-four dollars and ninety-four cents ($42,024.94). It is but just to say, however, that these institutions had at that time about one hundred and seventy-

PLATE II.

SILVER COINS OF THE UNITED STATES.

I. Half-Dollar—Fifty Cents.

II. One Dollar. 1870.

III. Twenty-Five Cents. 1870.

IV. One Dime. 1870.

V. Half-Dime.

VI. Three Cents.

PLATE II.

SILVER COINS OF THE UNITED STATES.

I. HALF-DOLLAR. 1870.

Authorized by Act of Congress, 1853.

WEIGHT, 192 Grains.

Fineness—900–1000.

Legal tender not exceeding five dollars.

II. ONE DOLLAR. 1870.

Authorized by Act of Congress, 1837.

WEIGHT, 412.5 Grains.

Fineness—900–1000.

III. TWENTY-FIVE CENTS—QUARTER-DOLLAR. 1870.

Authorized by Act of Congress, 1853.

WEIGHT, 96 Grains.

Fineness—900–1000.

Legal tender not exceeding five dollars.

IV. ONE DIME—TEN CENTS. 1870.

Authorized by Act of Congress, 1853.

WEIGHT, 38.4 Grains.

Fineness—900–1000.

V. HALF-DIME—FIVE CENTS. 1870.

Authorized by Act of Congress, 1853.

WEIGHT, 19.2 Grains.

Fineness—900–1000.

Legal tender not exceeding one dollar.

VI. THREE CENTS. 1870.

Authorized by Act of Congress, March 3, 1853.

WEIGHT, 11.52 Grains.

Fineness—900–1000.

five thousand dollars ($175,000) in Government Bonds, and loaned on call, with stock collaterals with which to meet emergencies, nearly all of which was in one institution. So far as I learn they all comply with the laws, but their charters are very peculiar and liberal. They are the legalized repository of trust funds of estates, courts, minors, guardians, etc.,—the most sacred characteristic which can possibly be given to any moneyed institution, and all they are required to do is to show their affairs to the Bank Commissioners when called upon. They are not required to advertise and swear to their condition as State banks proper are, nor are they required to keep any reserve for the protection of these minors, guardians, and trustees, for whom they are the legal custodians, as the old State banks were for the protection of billholders; but according to their charters they can start with a very small capital paid up, invest it, all and more, in real estate, and then borrow all the money they can, at a rate of interest agreed upon, and loan the last cent of it out, when, where, and to whom they choose. These companies are undoubtedly all safe and sound now, but there can be but one end to this loose sort of banking, if it should be carried to any considerable extent, and that must be disastrous.''

This appearing in a public State paper warrants us in quoting it, and giving to our friends who do business with us the following statement of our own strength in comparison with the strength of the Trust Companies. We do this in no boastful spirit, but merely to show our depositors and patrons that we believe in sound conservative banking, and that we keep ourselves in a strong position.

Our capital is over one hundred thousand dollars ($100,000), all in cash in our business; besides which, all the private property of the partners—which is quite large outside of the business—is holden. Our deposits are a little less than five hundred thousand dollars ($500,000), or less than one-half of the deposits in the Trust Companies, and yet our cash on hand during the six months preceding that message was as follows:

BALANCES IN BANKS AND ON HAND IN TILL.

1871.

Dec. 1. Balances in Banks................................ $117,524.03

Cash in Till.. 17,185.86

$134,709.89

1872.

Jan. 1. Balances in Banks................................ $43,329.28

Cash in Till.. 26,703.05

$70,032.33

Feb. 1. Balances in Banks................................ $237,963.70

Cash in Till.. 22,693.88

$260,657.58

March 1. Balances in Banks................................ $147,557.05

Cash in Till.. 18,586.18

$166,143.23

April 1. Balances in Banks................................ $67,977.24

Cash in Till.. 28,800.73

$96,777.97

May 1. Balances in Banks................................ $112,251.36

Cash in Till.. 41,777.84

$154,029.20

PLATE III.

THE GOLD COINS OF FRANCE.

I. 50 Francs. Napoleon III.—Value £ 1 19s. 7¾d.—$ 9 58.

II. 100 Francs. Napoleon III.—£ 3 19s. 3½d.—$ 19 16.

III. 40 Francs. Napoleon I.—£ 1 11s. 8½d.—$ 7 66.

IV. 20 Francs. Napoleon III.—15s. 10½d.—$ 3 83.

V. 10 Francs. Napoleon III.
7s. 11½d.--$ 1 92.

VI. 5 Francs. Napoleon III.
3s. 11½d.—96 cents.

PLATE III.

THE GOLD COINS, OF FRANCE.

I. 50 FRANCS.—NAPOLEON III. 1857.

WEIGHT, 248.908 Grains Troy—(16.129 Grammes).
Fineness—900-1000.
Value, £1 19s. 7¾d.—$ 9 58.

II. 100 FRANCS OF NAPOLEON III. 1859.

WEIGHT, 497.816 Grains Troy—(32.258 Grammes).
Fineness—900-1000.
Value, £3 19s. 3½d.—$ 19 16.

III. 40 FRANCS.—NAPOLEON I. 1812.

WEIGHT, 199.1235 Grains Troy—(12.903 Grammes).
Fineness—900-1000.
Value, £1 11s. 8⅝d.—$ 7 66.

IV. 20 FRANCS.—NAPOLEON III. 1861.

WEIGHT, 99.561 Grains Troy—(6.451 Grammes).
Fineness—900-1000.
Value, 15s. 10¼d.—$ 3 83.

V. 10 FRANCS.—NAPOLEON III. 1859.

WEIGHT, 49.769 Grains Troy—(3.225 Grammes).
Fineness—900-1000.
Value, 7s. 11⅛d.—$ 1 92.

VI. 5 FRANCS.—NAPOLEON III. 1858.

WEIGHT, 24.876 Grains Troy—(1.612 Gramme).
Fineness—900-1000.
Value, 3s. 11½d.—96 cents.

Thus it will be seen that we have at all times from one-third to one-half of the amount of our deposits on hand in cash.

We are not afraid to compare the above statement with that of any Bank or Trust Company in the Union. We will add that this has been our rule for a long time, and for years there has hardly been a day when we have not had over one hundred thousand dollars cash on hand and in Bank, and the daily average has been nearer two hundred thousand than one hundred thousand, not counting Government Bonds and call loans, of which we always have a large amount ready for instant use. We will further state that we have no part-due paper, or bad or slow debts.

We submit the above to our customers, confident that it will meet with their approval; and we assure them that as in the past we have kept strong, so in the future we shall endeavor at all times to keep well fortified.

In issuing this statement we disclaim any intention of trying to draw away depositors from Banks or Trust Companies. We send it to our friends only, that they may see for themselves that, in proportion to the magnitude of our liabilities, we are as sound as any Banking Institution in the State. We do not object to competition. In spite of the sharp competition and bidding for deposits by others during the past two years, our deposits have steadily and largely increased, and our business has been healthy and profitable beyond that of all former years.

The fundamental rule of our house, and one to which we always adhere, is *to steer clear of all speculation.* In the eighteen years of our history we have lived up to this mark, and the result has been not only our own steadily increasing prosperity and accumulation of capital in our business, but the growing confidence of our numerous customers and of the public at large.

We deal only in first-class, safe, and well-known securities, and we let all others alone.

Coin and U. S. Coupons

PURCHASED AT THE HIGHEST POSSIBLE PREMIUM.

Buying and Selling Stocks and Bonds.

Our facilities for buying and selling Stocks and Bonds at the Brokers' Board in New York, Boston, Hartford, and other cities, are unsurpassed.

Our correspondents in the large cities are of the most reliable character.

If you wish to buy or sell Hartford Stocks, or any other, you cannot do better than to call on us.

To persons wishing to dispose of Stocks or Bonds,

PLATE IV.
THE SILVER COINS OF FRANCE.

I. 5 Francs. Napoleon I.—Value, 4s. 0½d.—98 cents.

II. 5 Francs. Napoleon III.—4s. 0½d.—98 cents.

III. 2 Francs. Napoleon III.—1s. 7¾d.—36.4 cents.

IV. 1 Franc. Napoleon III.
9¾d.—18.2 cents.

V. 50 Centimes. Napoleon III.
4⅞d.—9.1 cents.

VI. 25 Centimes. Louis Philippe.
2¼d.—4½ cents.

VII. 20 Centimes. Napoleon III.
2d. . . . .

PLATE IV.

THE SILVER COINS OF FRANCE.

I. 5 FRANCS.—NAPOLEON I. 1812.
WEIGHT, 385.808 Grains Troy—(25 Grammes).
Fineness—900–1000.
Value, 4s. 0¼d.—98 cents.

II. 5 FRANCS.—NAPOLEON III. 1856.
WEIGHT, 385.808 Grains Troy—(25 Grammes).
Fineness—900–1000.
Value, 4s. 0½d.—98 cents.

III. 2 FRANCS.—NAPOLEON III. 1853.
WEIGHT, 154.323 Grains Troy—(10 Grammes).
Fineness—900–1000.
Value, 1s. 7¾d.—36.4 cents.

IV. 1 FRANC.—NAPOLEON III. 1860.
WEIGHT, 77.161 Grains Troy—(5 Grammes).
Fineness—900–1000.
Value, 9¾d.—18.2 cents.

V. 50 CENTIMES.—NAPOLEON III. 1858.
WEIGHT, 38.580 Grains Troy—(2.50 Grammes).
Fineness—900–1000.
Value, 4¾d.—9.1 cents.

VI. 25 CENTIMES.—LOUIS PHILIPPE. 1847.
WEIGHT, 19.29 Grains Troy—(1.25 Gramme).
Fineness—900–1000.
Value, 2¼d.—4½ cents.

VII. 20 CENTIMES.—NAPOLEON III. 1860.
WEIGHT, 15.432 Grains Troy—(1 Gramme).
Fineness—900–1000.
Value, 2d.

which have a marketable value, we offer the following terms: We pay the highest price which in our judgment we should be justified in offering under the ruling quotations; or we forward the securities to New York or Boston, or to any other market where they can be disposed of to the best advantage, for sale at such a limit as the owner may direct. In the latter case we deduct from the proceeds of the sale the actual expense incurred, such as expressage, etc., and the ordinary broker's commission. The seller may thus realize at once in cash, or by taking the risk of the market himself, may obtain, under favorable circumstances, a somewhat higher figure.

INVESTMENTS.

We deal largely in all kinds of first-class Stocks, Bonds, and Securities; and persons wishing to make investments, either temporarily or for a term of years, will find at our office, at all times, a large assortment from which to make a selection.

We particularly recommend the

NINE PER CENT. REAL ESTATE BONDS

which we offer, based upon first mortgages on first-class property in Western cities.

They are in the form of handsomely-printed Coupon

Bonds, having ten years to run. Interest Coupons, payable semi-annually, secured by trust deeds of first-class property, generally blocks of fine stores in such cities as Louisville, Indianapolis, Fort Wayne, Terre Haute, Grand Rapids, Evansville, and other first-rate growing railroad centres. Loans in all cases are for less than the land alone is worth, and the buildings must be good blocks, renting well, and well insured in solid companies. We have the property appraised, not by the friends and neighbors of the borrower, but by our own agent, a gentleman of large experience, who has been an agent of the old Ætna Insurance Company for thirty years, and who, in years of service for us, never made an over-appraisement; indeed, he always errs on the safe side.

There is no safer investment than a Bond and Mortgage; and a Bond and Mortgage, well selected, in any of the cities above named, is as good as one in Boston or Hartford, besides paying better interest.

Trust Deeds, such as we use, can be collected in sixty days, and that is better than foreclosing a mortgage at the East, where a long year of right of redemption is allowed. The Chicago fire tested the goodness of these loans. We had loaned large amounts there, and not a dollar was lost, and no payment of interest was delayed a day.

PLATE V.

ENGLISH GOLD COINS.

I. 5 Guineas. George II.—$ 25 50.

II. Guinea. George III.—$ 5 12.

III. 1–2 Guinea. George III.—$ 2 56.

IV. 1–3 Guinea. Geo. III.—$ 1 71. V. 1–4 Guinea. Geo. III.—$ 1 28.

VI. 2 Guineas. Charles II.—$ 10 25.

PLATE V.

ENGLISH GOLD COINS.

I. FIVE GUINEAS.—GEORGE II. 1729.

WEIGHT, 647.191 Grains Troy—(41.937 Grammes).

Fineness--22 Carats—916.66–1000.

Value, £5 5s. 0d.

II. GUINEA.—GEORGE III. 1798.

WEIGHT, 129.4382 Grains Troy—(8.3874 Grammes).

Value, £1 1s. 0d.

III. HALF GUINEA.—GEORGE III. 1810.

WEIGHT, 64.7191 Grains Troy—(4.1937 Grammes).

Value, £0 10s. 6d.

IV. 1–3 GUINEA.—GEORGE III. 1810.

WEIGHT, 43.146 Grains Troy—(2.7958 Grammes).

Value, £0 7s. . . . .

V. 1–4 GUINEA.—GEORGE III. 1762.

WEIGHT, 32.3595 Grains Troy—(2.0968 Grammes).

Value, £0 5s. 3d.

VI. TWO GUINEAS.—CHARLES II. 1684.

WEIGHT, 258.876 Grains Troy—(16.7748 Grammes).

Value, £2 2s. 0d.

We have sold this class of Bonds for the past twenty years. They have stood the test of panics, fires, and disasters, and never one failed; and no buyer ever sustained the loss of a cent, principal or interest. They are confidently recommended as a solid, tried security to all who desire an absolutely safe investment.

As we are receiving letters from all parts of the country inquiring about these Bonds, we give below such information, in a concise form, as occurs to us will be of value in deciding upon the merits of this security.

1st. The Property.

We never lend on farm-lands, or what is called "out property," of any kind. We take good central improved property, which in most cases is renting for more than the interest on the loan.

2d. How is it Appraised?

It is appraised by our own agent and attorney, a gentleman of rare ability and extreme caution, who is in our interest and who is bound to value it as low as possible, so as to be on the safe side. Then we have his valuations reviewed by bank officers and others, who are our friends and who must fully confirm the valuation of our agent, or we will not take the loan. Further, if desired at the time of purchasing the Bond,

we give the purchaser a memorandum allowing him six
months to make inquiries; and if in that time he finds
that the property is over-valued, we will take back the
Bond at par and accrued interest. We have given this
privilege in very many cases, and never yet had a Bond
returned; and where inquiries have been made, the in-
variable report has been that the property was worth
more than we stated it to be.

3d. Amount Loaned on Property.

We lend an amount less than the land alone is
worth. We require that fine buildings shall be upon
the property, well insured in companies which have
stood through Chicago and Boston fires: thus (while
we have good buildings well insured) we rely upon
the value of the land.

4th. Titles.

We require in all cases full abstracts of titles,
tracing the property back to the United States or State
title, and continuing down in unbroken succession.
This abstract we have certified to by the clerks of
courts and recorders of the counties where the property is located, and then besides all this we have it
carefully revised and searched by two good attorneys,
who give their written certificate of perfect title in fee

PLATE VI.

COINS OF GREAT BRITAIN.

I. Two Sovereigns.—William IV. 1831.—Value, £2 $9 72.

II. Five Sovereigns.—Queen Victoria. 1839.—Value, £5—$ 24 30.

III. Two Sovereigns.—George IV.—Value, £2—$ 9 72.

IV. Sovereign.—Victoria. 1861.—Value, £1—$ 4 86.

V. Half Sovereign.—Victoria. 1850.—Value, 10s.—$ 2 43.

PLATE VI.
COINS OF GREAT BRITAIN.

I. TWO SOVEREIGNS.— WILLIAM IV. 1831.

WEIGHT, 246.548 Grains Troy—(15.976 Grammes).

Fineness—916.66–1000.

Value, £2.—$9 72.

II. FIVE SOVEREIGNS.—VICTORIA.

WEIGHT, 616.372 Grains Troy—(39.9401 Grammes).

Fineness, 916.66–1000.

Value, £5—$24 10.

III. TWO SOVEREIGNS.—GEORGE IV. 1823.

WEIGHT, 246.548 Grains Troy—(15.976 Grammes).

Fineness, 916.66–1000.

Value, £2—$9 72.

IV. SOVEREIGN.—VICTORIA. 1861.

WEIGHT, 123.274 Grains Troy—(7.988 Grammes).

Fineness—916.66–1000.

Value, £1—$4 86.

V. HALF SOVEREIGN.—VICTORIA.

WEIGHT, 61.6372 Grains Troy—(3.994 Grammes).

Fineness—916.66–1000.

Value, 10s.—$2 43.

simple. In this matter of titles we take extraordinary precautions, and we never yet made a mistake.

5th. Time the Bonds have to Run.

The Bonds are in all cases ten-year Bonds, with the privilege given to the signer of the Bond to pay them any time after five years. They may thus be called Five-Ten Bonds. We have adopted this plan, as it allows a borrower to pay up his loan by degrees, which, in many cases, is more convenient than to raise a large sum at once. He is only allowed to pay Bonds in full which are drawn by lot, and not by partial payments on each. This adds to the strength of the Bonds which remain, as there is no release of any of the property till *all* are paid.

6th. In Case of Foreclosure.

In case of non-payment of interest (which but seldom happens, for in twenty years we have had to foreclose only two mortgages, and in each case the money came quickly without loss of a cent), any one Bondholder can direct a foreclosure, but he does it for all the Bondholders in common. No one or more Bondholder has any rights or preference over another. All share alike.

7th. For what can they be Foreclosed?

The Bonds, or deed, can be foreclosed for non-payment of interest promptly, or if the borrower neglects to keep his property insured in companies satisfactory to the trustee, who acts for the Bondholder, or if he allows anything to be done on the premises calculated to lessen its value (for example, if he pulls down a building, or lets it go to decay, or changes it from a store to a concert-saloon, or anything of that kind); for any of these causes foreclosure and sale can at once take place.

8th. The Deeds.

The deeds are Deeds of Trust drawn in the strongest manner. In twenty years' experience we have noticed and incorporated into our deeds all the strong points known to the law, and such documents have well been styled at the West "scalp mortgages." The borrower *must* pay. If he does not, no mercy is shown him. He is allowed sixty days' notice, and if at the end of that time he is delinquent, the property is sold at auction, and he pays all expenses, even to the lawyer's fees, of the Bondholder. The Bondholder is not at any expense for any proceeding. There is no stay, valuation, or appraisement law; and no right of redemption

PLATE VII.

SILVER COINS OF GREAT BRITAIN.

I. Four Pence.—Victoria. 1848.

II. Three Pence.—Victoria. 1861.

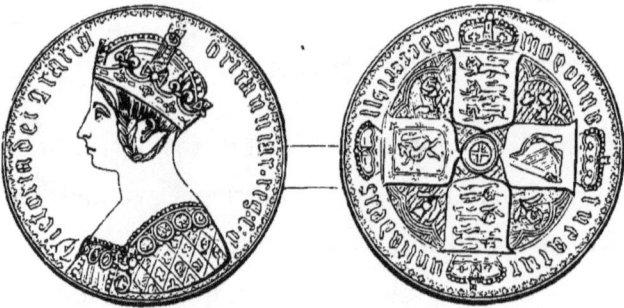

III. Crown.—Victoria. 1857. 5s.

IV. Two Pence.—George III. 1818.

V. Three Half-Pence.—Victoria. 1845.   VI. Penny.—Victoria. 1851.

PLATE VII.

COINS OF GREAT BRITAIN.

I. FOUR PENCE.—VICTORIA.

WEIGHT, 29.0909 Grains Troy—(1.88505 Gramme).

Fineness—925-1000.

II. THREE PENCE.—VICTORIA.

WEIGHT, 21.8181 Grains Troy—(1.4138 Gramme).

Fineness—925-1000.

III. CROWN.—VICTORIA. 1857.

WEIGHT, 436.3636 Grains Troy—(28.276 Grammes).

Fineness—925-1000.

Value, 5s.

IV. TWO PENCE.—GEO. III. 1818.

WEIGHT, 14.545 Grains Troy—(0.9425 Gramme).

Fineness—925-1000.

V. THREE HALF-PENCE.—VICTORIA. 1845.

So called MAUNDY MONEY.

WEIGHT, 10.909 Grains Troy—(0.707 Gramme).

VI. PENNY MAUNDY MONEY.—VICTORIA. 1851.

WEIGHT, 7.2725 Grains Troy—(0.47125 Gramme).

such as is common in our long-winded New England mortgages. Our deeds are the most perfect documents for strength and swiftness of execution that we have ever seen.

9th. The Bonds.

The Bonds are printed under our direction, on Bond paper furnished by ourselves, in sums of $1000 each, having coupons attached, which are payable semi-annually at our office. We remit for the coupons when paid, and also for the Bond at maturity when paid, by New York check, without charge to persons who reside out of Hartford. The name of the owner of the Bond can be written in the Bond, thus making it a registered security, good only to the owner, and perfectly safe to keep in the house. If the name of the owner is not written in, then the title passes by delivery like a Railroad or Government Bond.

10th. Mortgages are Safe.

These are in all cases first mortgages, and an experience of twenty years has convinced us that there is no investment so safe as a good first mortgage on good city property,—valuing the land moderately and lending a less amount than the land alone is worth. No mismanagement can affect such a loan. Railroad

Bonds may be injured by the mismanagement of the Directors of the Road. Town, country, and city Bonds may be repudiated by a vote of the people, as has often been done when the people get tired of paying taxes to keep up the interest. The goodness of Bank Stocks and manufacturing Stocks, and all other Stocks, in most cases depends upon the management of one or more men who control them; but if you have a first mortgage on a man's store or dwelling-house for an amount less than the land is worth under the hammer, he may fail and go to wreck generally, but the property remains, and somebody will take it and keep the interest and principal good. In these days of mismanagement it is well to have money invested where its safety does not depend upon any man's ability or integrity, or upon a vote of disaffected, irresponsible citizens. We claim this entire safety for our nine per cent. first mortgage Bonds.

11th. We take these Bonds Ourselves.

We do not sell these Bonds on Commission. In all cases as soon as the papers are made out and approved, we give our check for the Bonds, and they become our property. We are willing to put our own money into them, and we never sell a Bond which we would not willingly hold ourselves.

PLATE VIII.

SILVER COINS OF GREAT BRITAIN.

I. Half-Crown.—Victoria. 1845.
Value, 2s. 6d.

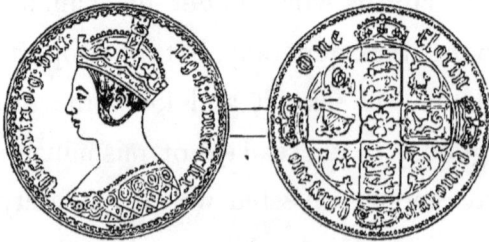

II. Florin.—Victoria. 1852.
Value, 2s.

III. Shilling.—Victoria. 1856.
Value, 1s.

IV. Sixpence.—Victoria. 1859.
Value, 6d.

PLATE VIII.

SILVER COINS OF GREAT BRITAIN.

I. HALF-CROWN.—VICTORIA. 1845.

WEIGHT, 218.1818 Grains Troy—(14.138 Grammes).

Fineness—925-1000.

Value, 2s. 6d.

II. FLORIN.—VICTORIA. 1852.

WEIGHT, 174.5454 Grains Troy—(11.3103 Grammes).

Fineness—925-1000.

Value, 2s.

III. SHILLING.—VICTORIA. 1856.

WEIGHT, 87.2727 Grains Troy—(5.655 Grammes).

Fineness—925-1000.

Value, 1s.

IV. SIXPENCE.—VICTORIA. 1859.

WEIGHT, 43.6363 Grains Troy—(2.828 Grammes.)

Fineness—925-1000.

Value, 6d.

12th. Who Invest in these Bonds?

We sell them to our most cautious business men and capitalists. Of course in a public circular like this we cannot give the names of buyers, but we can say in general terms that there is hardly a man of means in Hartford who does not own more or less of them. Many of our largest capitalists and shrewdest men have sold their Governments and bought these nine per cent. Bonds. Also, there is hardly a trust fund in this city which has not bought them largely. Our most cautious and sagacious business men are our best customers, and we sell them in large amounts all through New England, New York, Pennsylvania, Maryland, and as far west as Louisville. A list of the buyers taken from our books would be a list of the most prudent and cautious business men in this city, New England, and New York State.

13th. Loans are in Several Cities.

We make these loans in Indianapolis, Fort Wayne, Terre Haute, Evansville, Louisville, Grand Rapids, and several other Western cities, selecting only thriving, prosperous places, and taking only the best property. As we generally have an assortment of from one hundred thousand to two hundred and fifty thousand dollars of

Bonds actually on hand and paid for, and applications for as much more distributed through various localities, we can divide any sum which may seek investment so that it may not all be in one place.

14th. Loans Carefully Attended to.

We keep all the papers, deeds, policies, etc. in our vault; and during the continuance of the loan we look after its various details thoroughly. We keep the policies renewed in good companies. We attend to the payment of the coupons, and we have active correspondents in each of the cities, who at once inform us if any change is made adversely affecting the property. This part of our business is admirably systematized. We save the Bondholder from all care, thought, or anxiety, and holders of our nine per cent. Bonds may be assured that their interests will never suffer through any neglect of ours.

15th. Are these Loans readily Convertible into Cash ?

Of course a Bond or mortgage is never quite so quickly convertible into money as a Government Bond or a leading Railroad Bond ; but while on Government and Railroad Bonds one gets a low rate of interest, on these mortgages he gets a very high rate, and the

PLATE IX.

MEXICAN GOLD COINS.

I. Doblon or Doubloon.—Value $ 15 53.

II. 1-4 Doubloon.—$ 3 88.

III. 1-8th Doubloon.—$ 1 94.

IV. 1-16th Doubloon.—97 cents.

V. 1-2 Doubloon.—$ 7 76.

PLATE IX.

MEXICAN GOLD COINS.

I. DOBLOON or DOUBLOON —Onza De Oro. 1850.

WEIGHT, 417.707 Grains Troy—(27.067 Grammes).

Fineness, 875-1000.

Value, £3 4s. 8¼d.—$15 53 to $15 61.

II. QUARTER DOBLON.—1-4 Onza de Oro of 2 Escudos.
Year 1825.

WEIGHT, 104.430 Grains Troy—(6.767 Grammes).

Value, £0 16s. 2d.—$3 88 to $3 90.

III. EIGHTH DOBLON.—1-8 Onza de Oro
or Escudo of two Pesos. 1850.

WEIGHT, 52.207 Grains Troy—(3.382 Grammes).

Value, £0 8s. 1d.—$1 94 to $1 95.

IV. ONE-SIXTEENTH ONZA DE ORO. 1834.

WEIGHT, 26.111 Grains Troy—(1.692 Gramme).

Value, £0 4s. 0½d. — 97 to 98 cts.

V. HALF DOBLON.—1-2 Onza de Oro of 4 Escudos.

WEIGHT, 208.845 Grains Troy—(13.533 Grammes).

Fineness, 875-1000.

Value, £1 12s. 4½d.—$7 76 to $7 80.

difference more than pays for any slight difficulty in convertibility. We have found in our business that investors have often preferred Bonds which have run some little time and which have thus proved themselves good; and this demand for old Bonds has always been so great that we have been able to buy back all which have ever been presented at only a commission off, and thus investors who have desired to realize have found these Bonds readily convertible into cash, without any of the fluctuations and losses which are common to Stocks and other Bonds. For example, after the Chicago fire one of our Insurance Companies, which held a large amount of them, came to us, and we bought the lot at once, and the President remarked that "they were the most readily convertible security in their whole list of solid investments." But while we consider the Bonds as easy to realize on as Bank Stock or any other first-class security, besides not being subject to fluctuations in price, we prefer to sell to such persons only as wish an investment of a safe, permanent character.

Our Twenty Years' Experience of Great Value.

In speaking of the security of mortgages, it cannot be assumed that all mortgages offered by parties of little or no experience afford a safe investment. Judgment is required in the first selection of the property upon which the loan shall be made ; a nice discrimination as to the character of the man who receives the money ; disinterested appraisers, of experience, who are not neighbors and friends of the applicant, and who will set a valuation that will stand the test—if need be—of a sale under the hammer ; and, finally, a lawyer versed in real estate law, who will not take an abstract as satisfactory proof of clear title, but will investigate fully the record books, and look out for flaws which cannot be discovered in a hurried examination by one who has no other interest than simply to secure his fee. It is just here that we make our strongest claim. For twenty years we have given these points our closest study. Our agents, appraisers, and lawyers stand unrivaled in their respective departments ; our transactions are so large that we are able to secure their entire services, and their interests in making no mistakes are identical with ours. Such experience as ours, and such a trained corps of assistants as we have, cannot be obtained in a day nor in a year ; and we claim that our Bonds, gotten up under such auspices, cannot be equaled by those of any other Banking House or Association in the country.

We have thus given all the points which occur to us ; but we will be happy to answer any questions concerning these securities which may suggest themselves to those who wish to buy.

PLATE X.
THE COINS OF MEXICO.

I. 4 Reales de Plata—Half-Dollar. 1842.—Value, £0 2s. 2¼d.

II. Piaster of 8 Reales. 1856.—Value, £0 4s. 4⅝d.

III. 2 Reales de Plata—½ Dollar. 1861.—Value, £0 1s. 1⅛d.

IV. Real de Plata—⅛ Dollar. 1832.—Value, 6½d.

V. ½ Real de Plata.—Augustin. 1822.—Value, 3¼d.

PLATE X.

THE SILVER COINS OF MEXICO.

I. 4 REALES DE PLATA—1-2 Dollar. 1842.

WEIGHT, 208.845 Grains Troy—(13.533 Grammes).

Fineness—902.778–1000.

Value, £0 2s. 2¼d.—53 cts.

II. PESO, or PIASTER of 8 REALES DE PLATA. 1856.

WEIGHT, 417.707 Grains Troy—(27.067 Grammes).

Fineness—902,778–1000.

Value, £0 4s. 4⅝d.—$1 06.

III. 2 REALES DE PLATA—1-4 Dollar. 1861.

WEIGHT, 104.430 Grains Troy—(6.767 Grammes).

Fineness—902.778–1000.

Value, £0 1s. 1⅛d.—$0 26 cts.

IV. REAL DE PLATA—1-8 Dollar. 1832.

WEIGHT, 52.207 Grains Troy—(3.383 Grammes).

Fineness—902.778–1000.

Value, 6½d.—13 cts.

V. 1-2 REAL DE PLATA.—AUGUSTIN. 1822.

WEIGHT, 26.111 Grains Troy—(1.692 Gramme).

Fineness—902.778–1000.

Value, 3¼d.—6½ cts.

In summing up we can only say, that if these Bonds are not good then we do not know what is. We have sold immense amounts during twenty years without the loss of a cent to our customers or ourselves. We shall take as much care in the future as in the past, and we ask, What can be better, as an investment, than these

Nine Per Cent. Bonds?

We Refer to

Hartford National Bank . . . . Hartford.

Exchange National Bank . . . . . "

Farmers' and Mechanics' National Bank . "

Hon. Calvin Day . . . . . . "

Bank of New York . New York.

Vermilye & Co. . . . "

NEW YORK CITY BANK STOCKS.

BANKS.	CAPITAL.	SHARES.	DIVIDEND MONTHS.	DIVIDENDS.
American Exchange..	$5,000,000	100	May, Nov.	4 × 4
Atlantic	300,000	75	Jan., July.	4 × 4
America	3,000,000	100	" "	5 × 5
Bowery	250,000	100	" "	5 × 5
Broadway	1,000,000	25	Quarterly.	12 × 12
Bull's Head	200,000	25	" "	5×5×5×5
Butchers' and Drovers'	800,000	25	Jan., July.	5 × 5
Bank of the State..	2,000,000	100	May, Nov.	4 × 4
Bank of New York..	2,000,000	100	Jan., July.	5 × 5
Bank of Commerce..	10,000,000	100	" "	4 × 4
Bank of North America	1,000,000	100	" "	3½× 3½
Bank of Com'nwealth.	750,000	100	" "	3 × 3
Bank of Republic	2,000,000	100	Feb., Aug.	4 × 4
Chemical	300,000	100	Jan., July.	4 × 4
Continental	2,000,000	100	Feb., Aug.	4 × 4
Corn Exchange	1,000,000	100	Jan., July.	8 × 4
Chatham	450,000	25	" "	5 × 4
Citizens	400,000	25	" "	5 × 5
City	1,000,000	100	May, Nov.	10 × 10
East River	350,000	25	Jan., July.	4 × 4
Fulton	600,000	30	May, Nov.	4 × 4
Gallatin	1,500,000	50	April, Oct.	4 × 4
Gold Exchange	500,000	100		
Greenwich	200,000	25	May, Nov.	10 × 10
Grocers'	300,000	50	Jan., July.	5 × 5
Hanover	1,000,000	100	" "	4 × 4
Importers' & Traders'.	1,500,000	100	" "	6 × 6
Irving	500,000	50	" "	4 × 6
Leather Manufacturers'	600,000	100	Feb., Aug.	6 × 6
Manhattan Company..	2,050,000	50	" "	6 × 6
Manufac. & Merchants'	500,000	100	Jan., July.	4 × 4
Marine	400,000	100	" "	6 × 4
Market	1,000,000	100	" "	5 × 5
Mechanics'	2,000,000	25	" "	5 × 5

BANKS.	CAPITAL.	SHARES.	DIVIDEND MONTHS.	DIVIDENDS.
Mech'cs' Bank'g Ass'n	$500,000	50	May, Nov.	4 × 4
Mechanics' & Traders'	600,000	25	" "	5 × 5
Mercantile	1,000,000	100	" "	5 × 5
Merchants'	3,000,000	50	Jan., July.	4 × 4
Merchants'	1,235,000	50	" "	3 × 3
Merchants' Exchange..	1,000,000	100	" "	5 × 5
Metropolitan	4,000,000	100	" "	5 × 5
Nassau	1,000,000	100	May, Nov.	4 × 3
New York County	200,000	100	Jan., July.	8 × 8
North River	400,000	100	" "	4 × 3
Ocean	1,000,000	50		
Oriental	300,000	25	Jan., July.	6 × 6
Pacific	422,700	50	Quarterly.	4×4×4×4
People's	412,500	25	Jan., July.	5 × 5
Park	2,000,000	100	" "	7 × 6
Phenix	1,800,000	20	" "	3½× 3½
Seventh Ward	500,000	100	" "	4 × 4
St. Nicholas	1,000,000	100	Feb., Aug.	5 × 5
Shoe and Leather	1,200,000	100	Jan., July.	6 × 6
Tradesmen's	1,000,000	40	" "	6 × 6
Union	1,500,000	50	May, Nov.	5 × 5
American National	500,000	100		
Central National	3,000,000	100	Jan., July.	4 × 4
First National	500,000	100	Quarterly.	5×5×5×5
Second National	300,000	100	Jan., July.	5 × 5
Third National	1,000,000	100	" "	4 × 4
Fourth National	5,000,000	100	" "	4 × 4
Fifth National	150,000	100	" "	4 × 4
Sixth National	200,000	100	" "	6 × 6
N. Y. National Exch..	500,000	100	" "	
National Currency	100,000	100	" "	6 × 6
Eighth National	250,000	100	" "	3½
Ninth National	1,500,000	100	Jan., July.	5 × 4
Tenth National	1,000,00C	100	" "	4 × 4

PLATE XI.

THE GOLD COINS OF PRUSSIA.

I. Krone (Crown).—Friedrich Wm. IV. 1859.—Value, £1 7s. 3¾d.

II. 2 Friedrichs d'or.—Friedrich Wm. IV. 1848.—Value, £1 12s. 11½d.

III. Friedrichs d'or.—Friedrich Wilhelm III. 1831.—Value, £0 16s. 5¾d.

IV. 1-2 Krone.—Friedrich Wm. IV. 1858.—Value, £0 13s. 7¾d.

V. 1-2 Friedrichs d'or.—Friedrich Wm. III. 1839.—Value, £0 8s. 2⅞d.

PLATE XI.

GOLD COINS OF PRUSSIA.

I. KRONE (CROWN) OF FRIEDRICH WILHELM IV. 1859.

Weight, 171.467 Grains Troy—(11.111 Grammes.)

Fineness—900-1000.

Value, £ 1 7*s*. 3¾*d*.

II. 2 FRIEDRICHS D'OR.—FRIEDRICH WILHELM IV. 1848.

Weight, 206.221 Grains Troy--(13.363 Grammes).

Fineness—902.778-1000.

Value, £ 1 12*s*. 11½*d*.

III. FRIEDRICHS D'OR.—FRIEDRICH WILHELM III. 1831.

Weight, 103.110 Grains Troy—(6.682 Grammes).

Fineness—902.778-1000.

Value, £ 0 16*s*. 5¾*d*.

IV. 1-2 KRONE, OF FRIEDRICH WILHELM IV. 1858.

Weight, 85.733 Grains Troy—(5.556 Grammes).

Fineness—900-1000.

Value, £0 13*s*. 7¾*d*.

V. 1-2 FRIEDRICHS D'OR.—FRIEDRICH WILHELM III. 1839.

Weight, 51.55 Grains Troy—(3.341 Grammes).

Fineness—902.778-1000.

Value, £0 8*s*. 2⅞*d*.

RAILROAD STATISTICS.

INCLUDING

Number of Miles, Stock, Bonds, Cost per Mile, Net Earnings, Dividends, Etc.

NAME OF RAILROAD.	NO. OF MILES.	STOCKS.	BONDS.	COST PER MILE.	NET EARNINGS.	DIVIDENDS.	WHEN PAYABLE	PAR.
Albany and Susquehanna	142	4,000,000	4,399,000	59,149	267,487		Jan and July	
Atlantic and Great Western	425	50,000,000	59,000,000	236,473	675,340		Jan and July	50
Baltimore and Ohio	411	16,681,762	11,186,185	67,805	4,006,503		Apr and Oct	100
Boston, Hartford and Erie	113	25,000,000	28,549,163	473,886	135,334			
Boston and Albany	250	19,664,100	821,500	81,542	2,154,983	10 per cent.	May and Nov	100
Boston and Providence	59	3,950,000		66,949	430,461	10 per cent.	Jan and July	100
Central Pacific	1401	54,283,190	82,208,000	97,421	5,220,914		Jan and July	100
Chicago, Rock Island and Pacific	544	19,000,000	8,698,000	50,915	3,171,535	8 per cent.	Apr and Oct	100
Chicago and Northwestern	1224	35,135,973	18,049,000	43,452	5,383,408		June and Dec	100
Chicago, Burlington and Quincy	706	18,664,324	4,555,350	32,747	3,004,707		Mch and Sept	100
Chicago and Alton	360	11,355,300	4,508,000	44,064	2,198,085	10 per cent.	Mch and Sept	100
Columbus, Chicago and Ind. Central	588	13,000,000	23,230,174	61,616	1,040,232		Quarterly	100
Central New Jersey	74	16,182,150	4,994,000	286,434	3,035,235	10 per cent.	Jan and July	100
Clev., Colum., Cincin. & Indianapolis	390	12,791,350	3,008,000	40,511	1,162,829	7 per cent.	Feb and Aug	100
Cleveland and Pittsburg	199	7,867,950	3,859,500	58,932	1,412,174	10 per cent.	Quarterly	50
Delaware, Lackawanna and Western	450	18,858,850	5,744,000	54,673	1,549,693	10 per cent.	Jan and July	50
Dubuque and Sioux City	143	5,000,000	894,000	41,216	301,344		Jan and July	100
Erie	588	86,536,910	26,398,800	192,068	1,895,404		Feb and Aug	100
Hannibal and St. Joseph	277	9,254,924	9,508,000	67,772	1,089,035	12 per cent.	Feb and Aug	100
Hartford and New Haven*	78	5,000,000	754,900	73,780	597,232	12 per cent.	Quarterly	100
Housatonic	74	2,000,000	391,000	32,319	92,384	12 per cent.	Jan and July	100

Indianapolis, Cincin. and Lafayette	179	7,685,497	9,648,017	96,835	622,313	7 per cent.	Feb and Aug	100
Illinois Central	707	25,280,510	8,394,500	47,630	2,732,847	8 per cent.	Quarterly	100
Joliet and Chicago	38	1,500,000	500,000	52,631			Feb and Aug	100
Lake Shore and Michigan Southern	1074	50,000,000	34,729,000	78,900	5,018,169		May and Sept	50
Marietta and Cincinnati	284	13,980,080	11,077,873	88,232	210,055		Jan and July	100
Michigan Central	285	17,987,048	7,233,989	88,495	1,506,424		Jan and July	100
Milwaukee and St. Paul	1018	22,649,215	18,151,339	40,079	2,840,341	7 per ct. pref.	Jan and July	100
Missouri, Kansas and Texas	592	16,257,500	20,250,000	61,668				
Morris and Essex	118	13,698,250	11,614,000	214,510	668,914	7 per cent.	Jan and July	100
New Jersey R.R. and Canal Co.	456	18,991,627	17,615,607	80,279	1,070,766		Apr and Oct	100
New York Central and Hudson	740	89,428,330	15,231,719	141,432	8,266,817	8 per cent.	Jan and July	100
New York and New Haven	62	7,500,000	1,061,000	138,080	903,346	10 per cent.	Jan and July	100
New Jersey Southern	86	4,000,000	2,870,000	79,884	165,004		Jan and July	100
New London and Northern	100	1,003,500	699,000	17,025	138,598	8 per cent.	Jan and July	100
Norwich and Worcester	66	2,823,400	759,000	54,278	261,747	10 per cent.	Mch and Sept	100
St. Louis, Kansas City and Northern	354	24,030,000	6,000,000	84,746	633,528		Jan and July	100
New York and Harlem	133	8,500,000	6,717,725	114,419	1,029,087	8 per cent.	June and Dec	100
Ohio and Mississippi	393	24,030,000	6,534,850	77,773	798,212		June and Dec	100
Pennsylvania Central	424	41,339,475	48,732,595	212,457	6,896,404		Quarterly	100
Pittsburg, Fort Wayne and Chicago	369	19,714,286	13,663,000	90,374	4,046,644	10 per cent.	Mch and Sept	100
Pacific of Missouri	284	3,635,750	11,200,000	52,239	947,801	7 per cent.	Jan and July	100
Panama	48	7,000,000	2,993,178	208,191	245,661	5 per cent.	Jan and July	100
Philadelphia and Reading	336	31,566,575	21,403,200	157,648	5,006,940	10 per cent.	Jan and July	50
St. Louis and Iron Mountain	258	10,000,000	4,000,000	54,264	667,320		Jan and July	100
St. Louis, Alton and Terre Haute	219	4,768,400	7,000,000	53,737	216,966		Annually	100
Toledo, Wabash and Western	606	16,000,000	17,704,000	55,615	1,959,837		May and Nov	100
Toledo, Peoria and Warsaw	246	5,700,000	6,450,000	45,325	400,000		May and Nov	100
Union Pacific	1032	36,745,000	76,166,512	109,410	3,921,115		Jan and July	100
Ware River	50	1,000,000	750,000	35,000	16,315		Jan and July	100

* Now consolidated with New York and New Haven.

PLATE XII.
THE COINS OF PRUSSIA.

I. Vereins-Thaler of Wilhelm. 1859.—Value, £0 2s. 11⅞d.

II. Two Vereins-Thaler of Wilhelm. 1861.—Value, £0 6s.

III. Vereins-Thaler of Friedrich Wilhelm IV. 1857.—Value, £0 2s. 11⅞d.

IV. 1-6 Thaler.—Value, 6d.

V. 2½ Silbergroschen.—Value, 2¾d.

VI. Silbergroschen.—Value, 1d.

VII. Half Silbergroschen.—½d.

PLATE XII.

SILVER COINS OF PRUSSIA.

I. VEREINS-THALER OF WILHELM. 1859.

Weight, 285.784 Grains Troy—(18.5185 Grammes).

Fineness—900–1000.

Value, £0 2s. 11⅞d.

II. 2 VEREINS-THALER OF WILHELM. 1861.

Weight, 571.568 Grains Troy—(37.0370 Grammes).

Fineness—900–1000.

Value, £0 6s. 0d.

III. VEREINS-THALER OF FRIEDRICH WILHELM IV. 1857.

Weight, 285.784 Grains Troy—(18.5185 Grammes).

Fineness—900–1000.

Value, £0 2s. 11⅞d.

IV. 1-6TH THALER OF WILHELM. 1862.

Weight, 82.438 Grains Troy—(5.342 Grammes).

Fineness—520–1000.

Value, £0 0s. 6d.

V. 2 1-2 SILBERGROSCHEN—WILHELM. 1862.

Weight, 49.708 Grains Troy—(3.221 Grammes).

Fineness—375–1000.

Value, £0 0s. 2¾d.

VI. 1 SILBERGROSCHEN.—WILHELM. 1861.

Weight, 33.873 Grains Troy—(2.195 Grammes).

Fineness—220–1000.

Value, £0 0s. 1d.

VII. 1-2 SILBERGROSCHEN OF FRIEDRICH WILHELM IV. 1856.

Weight, 16.913 Grains Troy—(1.096 Gramme).

Fineness—222.222–1000.

Value, £0 0s. ½d.

NEW COINS OF THE WORLD,

FAC-SIMILES OF WHICH ARE CONTAINED IN

The Banker's Almanac for 1873.

ONE VOLUME OCTAVO.   PRICE, THREE DOLLARS.

PLATE XVII.*—Great Britain—Sweden.

YEAR.	COUNTRY.	SOVEREIGN.	NAME.	WEIGHT.	FINENESS.	VALUE.
1872.....	Great Britain	Victoria.............	Sovereign.........	.256.6	916.5	$4.86
1872.....	Great Britain	Victoria.............	Sovereign.........	.256.6	916.5	4.86
1871.....	Canada.........	Victoria.............	Fifty Cents......	.375	925	0.47.2
1871.....	Sweden.........	Charles XV.......	Four Riksdaler.	1.092	750	1.11.5

PLATE XVIII.

1871.....	Germany	William	Ten Marks.......	.128	900	2.38
1872.....	Germany	William	Twenty Marks..	.256	900	4.76
1869.....	Wurtemberg ..	Karl, Koenig......	Double Thaler..	1.190	900	1.46
1869.....	Mexico...........	Republic...........	Peso..............	.867.5	903	1.06.5

PLATE XIX.—France.

1872.....	France	Republic...........	Two Francs......	.320	835	0.36.4
1871.....	France	Republic...........	Five Francs......	.800	900	0.98
1872.....	France	Republic...........	One Franc........	.160	835	0.18.2
1871.....	France	Republic...........	Fifty Centimes..	.80	835	0.09.1

PLATE XX.—Austria—Russia.

1871.....	Austria.........	Francis Joseph...	Four Ducats......	.448	986	9.13
1871.....	Austria.........	Francis Joseph...	Union-Thaler....	.596	900	0.73
1869.....	Hungary.......	Francis Joseph...	Florin..............	.397	900	0.48.5
1870.....	Russia...........	Alexander II.....	20 Copecks	.11.2	875	0.13.3

PLATE XXI.—Spain—Portugal.

1871.....	Spain............	Amadeo I..........	Five Pesetas......	.800	900	0.98
1870.....	Spain............	Republic...........	Five Pesetas......	.800	900	0.98
1871.....	Portugal	Ludovico I........	5000 Reis..........	.308	912	5.80.5
1871.....	Portugal	Ludovico I........	500 Reis..........	.400	912	0.49.6

PLATE XXII.—Italy—Denmark—Netherlands.

1869.....	Italy.............	Victor Emanuel..	Five Lire..........	.800	900	0.98
1869.....	States of Ch'h.	Pius IX............	Two Lire..........	.320	835	0.36.4
1868.....	Denmark	Christian IX......	Two Rigsdaler..	.927	877	1.10.7
1869.....	Netherlands...	William III.......	2½ Guilders......	.804	944	1.03

PLATE XXIII.—Japan.

1872.....	Japan.........	....	One Yen...........	.866	900	1.00.8
1872.....	Japan.........	....	Fifty Sen.........	.402	800	0.44.6
1872.....	Japan.........	....	Twenty Sen......	.160.8	800	0.17.8
1872.....	Japan.........	....	Ten Sen	.80.4	800	0.08.9

PLATE XXIV.—Japan.

1872.....	Japan.........	....	Five Sen	.40.2	800	0.04
1872.....	Japan.........	....	Twenty Yen......	1.072	900	19.94
1872.....	Japan.........	....	Five Yen..........	.268	900	4.93.5
1872.....	Japan.........	....	Two Yen..........	.107	900	1.99.4
1872.....	Japan.........	....	One Yen...........	.53.5	900	0.99.5

* Plates I. to XVI., containing Fac-similes, Weights, Values, etc., of Ninety-One Gold and Silver Coins of the UNITED STATES, GREAT BRITAIN, FRANCE, PRUSSIA, RUSSIA, SPAIN, and MEXICO, may be found in "THE COIN BOOK OF THE WORLD." (Edited by I. SMITH HOMANS.) One volume octavo. Price, $2.50.

www.ingramcontent.com/pod-product-compliance
Lightning Source LLC
Chambersburg PA
CBHW022023190326
41519CB00010B/1579